NAILED IT!

Extreme TIGHT-ROPE

Virginia Loh-Hagan

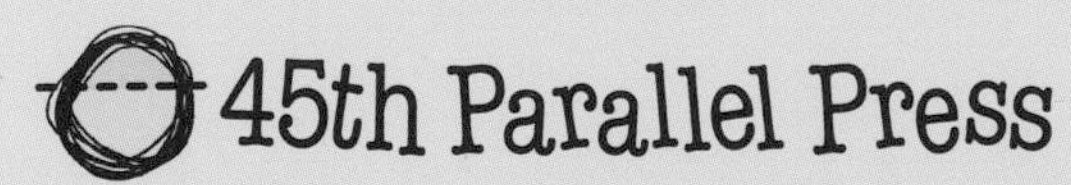

Published in the United States of America by Cherry Lake Publishing
Ann Arbor, Michigan
www.cherrylakepublishing.com

Content Adviser: Liv Williams, Editor, www.iLivExtreme.com
Reading Adviser: Marla Conn, ReadAbility, Inc.
Photo Credits: ©Vernon Wiley/istockphoto.com, cover, 1; ©JaredAlden/istockphoto.com, 5; ©GIAN EHRENZELLER/EPA/Newscom, 6; ©Małgorzata Paulina Pakuła/Dreamstime.com, 8; ©Anthony Correia/Shutterstock.com, 11; ©RFarrarons/Shutterstock.com, 12; ©thinair28/Shutterstock.com, 15; ©ZJAN/Credit Discovery Channel/Newscom, 17; ©JaredAlden/istockphoto.com, 19; ©FRED THORNHILL/Reuters/Corbis, 21; ©id1974/depositphotos, 23; ©Bettmann/Corbis, 24; ©Sergei Bachlakov/Shutterstock.com, 27; ©Alain Lacroix/Dreamstime.com, 29; ©Trusjom/Shutterstock.com, multiple interior pages; ©Kues/Shutterstock.com, multiple interior pages

45th Parallel Press is an imprint of Cherry Lake Publishing.

Library of Congress Cataloging-in-Publication Data

Loh-Hagan, Virginia.
Extreme tightrope / by Virginia Loh-Hagan.
pages cm. -- (Nailed it!)
Includes bibliographical references and index.
ISBN 978-1-63470-489-2 (hardcover) -- ISBN 978-1-63470-549-3 (pdf) -- ISBN 978-1-63470-609-4 (paperback) -- ISBN 978-1-63470-669-8 (ebook)
1. Tightrope walking--Juvenile literature. 2. Extreme sports--Juvenile literature. I. Title.
GV551.L65 2016
796.46--dc23

2015026125

ABOUT THE AUTHOR

Dr. Virginia Loh-Hagan is an author, university professor, former classroom teacher, and curriculum designer. The only time she walks on ropes is when she gets tangled in her dogs' leashes. She lives in San Diego with her very tall husband and very naughty dogs. To learn more about her, visit www.virginialoh.com.

Table of Contents

1

Walking High

What is high wire walking? What are the three types of high wire walking? Who is Marco Polo? Who is Freddy Nock? Who is Aisikaier Wubulikasimu?

Marco Polo stayed balanced. He waved. He walked across the ropes outside of **the big top**. It's the main **circus** tent. A circus is a traveling show. Tightrope walkers usually perform inside tents. Not Polo.

His tightrope walking acts are a hit. He balances on chairs. He fakes slipping. He wears washing baskets on his feet. He performs 10 times a week.

Polo is from Mexico. He said, "Circuses run in the family.

I was always interested in the **high wire**." High wire is walking on a tightrope in high places. It can be done anywhere. Wire just needs to be stretched between two points.

Tightrope walking in a circus is **artificial**. This means man-made. Wires are strung between poles. It's a type of high wire walking.

High wire walkers are at least 20 feet (6 m) above ground.

Tightrope walkers study nature. Freddy Nock had to get used to the mountain air.

Freddy Nock walked across a tightrope. He walked between two mountaintops. He walked across cable-car wires. He was 9,800 feet (2,987 meters) high. He set records. He had the highest tightrope walk. He crossed over 1,000 feet (305 m). He didn't use supports. He crossed in 39 minutes. He said, "I was not scared. The important thing is to feel the wire."

Nock practiced **natural** high wire walking. These tightrope walkers use objects in nature. They walk across valleys, waterfalls, and mountains. It's also called skywalking.

NAILED IT!

Spotlight Biography: Adili Wuxor

Adili Wuxor is the "Prince of Tightrope Walking." He started at age eight. He doesn't use safety gear. He said, "In my family's 450 years of history as tightrope walkers, we have never once used a safety rope." At age 20, he almost died. His rope snapped. He fell 65 feet (20 m). He broke 17 bones. He started tightrope walking again. He walks on long, steel wires now. He has several world records. He spent 60 days walking on a tightrope. He crossed mountain valleys. He crossed rivers. He danced. He walked blindfolded. He walked across a 5,020-foot-long (1,530 m) tightrope. He was 2,172 feet (662 m) high. He walked over another tightrope walker. They met midair. They were 853 feet (260 m) high. Their tightrope was 1,082 feet (330 m) long. It was stretched between two buildings. Wuxor learned from his father. His daughter is learning from him.

Tightrope walkers walk between city structures.

Nock's family began tightrope walking in 1770. Nock trained on tightropes at age three. He got married on a tightrope.

Aisikaier Wubulikasimu does natural high wire walking. He walked across a **ravine**. A ravine is a narrow canyon. He was 650 feet (198 m) high. He felt faint. The wind threw him off. He fell off the high wire. Rescuers found him. He had small injuries. He keeps walking tightrope.

He also does **architectural** high wire walking. This is using buildings or other man-made structures. He walked between two tall buildings. The tightrope was 328 feet (100 m) long. It took about six minutes. He was 500 feet (152.4 m) high. He got a world record. He also did the longest blindfolded tightrope walk.

He got another world record. He holds the quickest time crossing a high wire between two hot air balloons. He did it in 38.35 seconds.

2

Walking on Wire

What are the different types of tightrope walking? What is slacklining? What are some skills of tightrope walkers? How do tightrope walkers train?

High wire walking is one type of tightrope walking. Ropes are brass or steel cable. A pole helps them balance. A "death walk" is an extreme high wire walking move. It's walking at an angle.

Tightwire walking is another type. It's walking across a low, tight wire or rope. Tightwire includes dancing and props. Tightwire walkers don't have to use poles. They spread their arms out. Sarah Schwarz does tightwire. She plays with her hat. She tugs at the wire with her toes. She makes music.

Slacklining is a type of rope walking. **Slack** means loose. It's different from tightrope walking. Slacklining uses a loose, flat rope. Faith Dickey does slacklining. She walked between two moving trucks.

Tightrope walkers are **acrobats**. Acrobats perform gymnastics. They must maintain balance. It's difficult to balance on something hard. A rope adds motion. Balancing

High wire walkers use a pole to help balance.

on rope is even harder. Tightrope walkers must move with the rope. They position their body. They spread out their weight. They put one foot in front of the other.

They have special training. They train for years. They train in bad weather. They train in high winds. They train in snow and rain. They train their bodies to react to changes. They build strength. They build muscle. They practice walking at different heights. They practice walking different lengths.

NAILED IT!

Advice from the Field: Helen Skelton

Helen Skelton likes extreme sports. Tightrope walking was her "hardest challenge." She was the first person to walk between the chimneys of Battersea Power Station. It's in London. She walked on a high wire. She used a 26-foot-long (8 m) pole. The pole wobbled. She walked 492 feet (150 m). She did it in 11 minutes. She was 217 feet (66 m) high. Her stunt was delayed because of high winds. She trained in France. She tells others to work through fear. She also says to trust coaches. She said, "The first five or six steps, it didn't feel steady. I thought 'I can't do this' and I wanted to go back. Then my coach shouted out, 'It is gonna get easier.' And I thought, 'I have trusted you to this point. I will carry on trusting you.'"

Tightrope walkers wear special shoes. The shoes have leather bottoms. The wire digs into their feet. Tightrope walkers can curve their feet around the wire. The shoes also protect their feet. Some walk barefoot. Their toes grab the rope. The tightrope is rope or **braided** wire. Braided means woven together.

Extreme tightrope walkers don't use safety gear. They feel safety gear takes away from the sport. Part of the thrill is that they could fall. But they feel safe. They train. They prepare.

"Extreme tightrope walkers don't use safety gear."

Tightrope walkers study their locations.
They choose their gear to fit the stunt.

3

Defying Death

Who is Nik Wallenda? What happened to his family? What are some of his stunts? What does he think about safety gear?

Extreme tightrope walkers could hurt themselves. They could die.

Nik Wallenda holds several world records. His family is known as "The Flying Wallendas." They're a circus family. His mother walked tightropes while pregnant with him. They specialize in the high wire. They know about risks and dangers.

Their famous act was the seven-person chair **pyramid**.

A pyramid has a triangle shape. Seven tightrope walkers come out. They stand on each other. At the top, a tightrope walker sat on a chair. One of them was a new performer. He lost his balance. They all fell. Three tightrope walkers fell 35 feet (10.6 m). Two died. Some got hurt.

The show must go on! Nik Wallenda keeps tightrope walking. He walked across the Grand Canyon. He walked across Niagara Falls. He hung from a helicopter. He does crazy stunts.

Nik Wallenda is a daredevil tightrope walker.

That Happened?!?

Xiaoyan is a three-year-old girl. Some say she's the world's youngest tightrope walker. She walked across a tightrope. She was at a zoo in China. The rope was 164 feet (50 m) long. She wobbled. She was on one foot. Her arms were spread out. She tried to balance. She was 29 feet (9 m) above ground. There were nine tigers below her. They looked up at her. She was blown off the rope. She was pushed by high winds. People screamed. Her safety gear saved her. She was attached to a harness. A harness is a set of straps. It was attached to the rope. Xiaoyan's father said his daughter has been walking the tightrope since age one.

He walked on a Ferris wheel. It was still spinning. He got into his cart. He got to the top. He climbed out. He walked the outer rim. He worried more about weather than walking. Damp weather makes the parts wet. He said, "I don't want to slip."

He thinks about falling. He studies the weather. He over-prepares. He trains six hours a day. He trains six days a week.

Wallenda got two world records. He did the steepest tightrope slope between two buildings. He did the highest tightrope walk while blindfolded.

Tightrope walkers pay attention to the weather. Wind could push them off the rope.

He won't use a balancing pole. He won't use a safety net. He won't use supports. So far, he hasn't had a bad accident. He broke a toe playing football. That's his worst injury. He said, "My great-grandfather taught that safety nets offer a false sense of security." His uncle fell into a safety net. He died.

Wallenda relies on his skill. He said, "Walking the wire to me is life."

"Walking the wire to me is life."

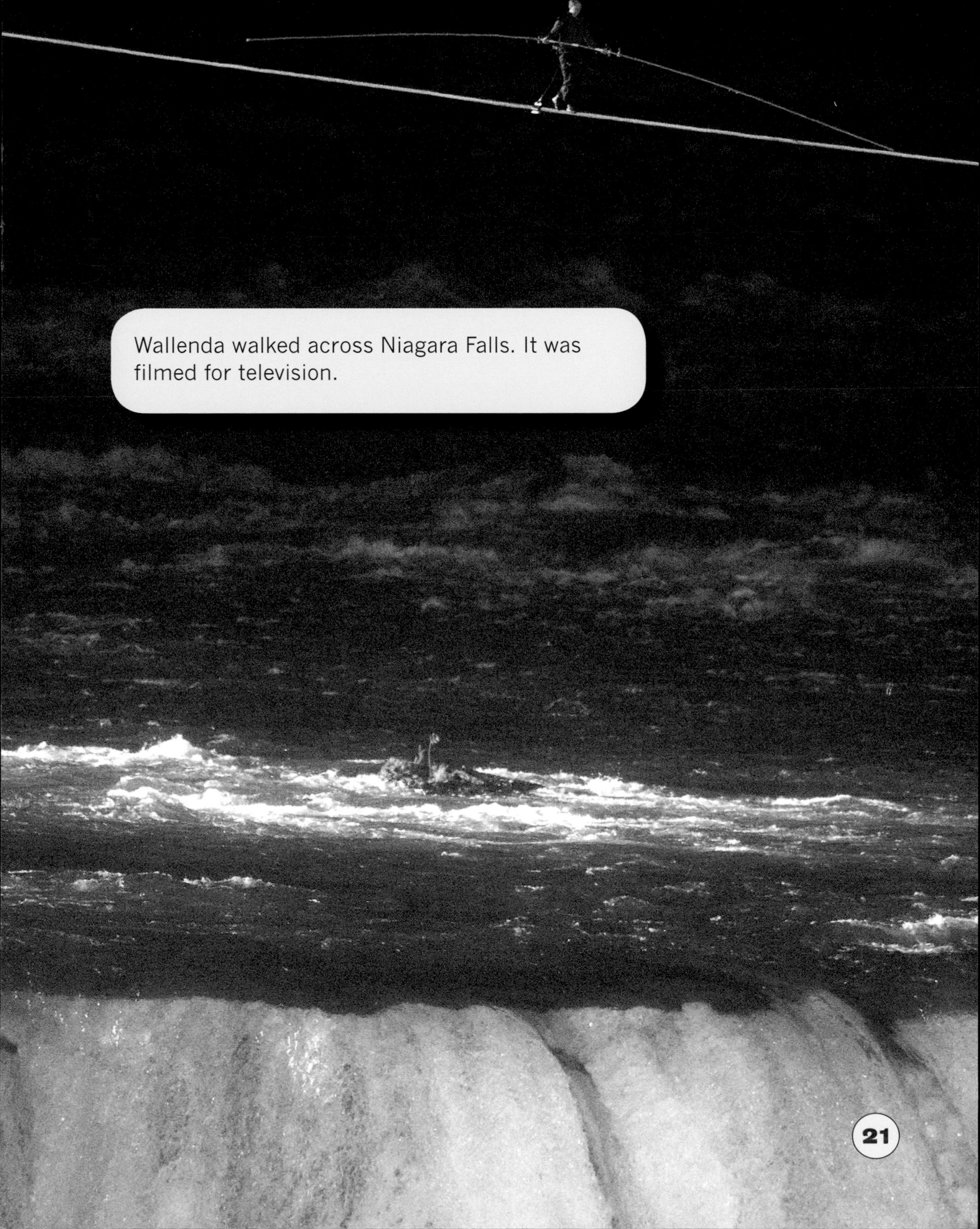

Wallenda walked across Niagara Falls. It was filmed for television.

4

Long History of Tightrope Walking

How did tightrope walking develop? Who is Madame Saqui? Who is Pablo Fanque? Who is "The Great Blondin"? Who is Philippe Petit?

Tightrope walkers entertained ancient Greeks and Romans. French and English royalty featured them in celebrations.

Madame Saqui lived in the late 1700s. She performed for Napoleon Bonaparte. Bonaparte was a French leader. Madame Saqui walked with fireworks. She walked between towers. She owned a circus theater.

Circuses became popular. Pablo Fanque was the first person of color to own a circus in Great Britain. He was a tightrope walker. He promoted tightrope walking.

Jean François Gravelet was "The Great Blondin." He was the first to cross Niagara Falls. He did it in 1859. He crossed several times. He did tricks each time. He sat down. He rode a bike. He cooked eggs. He walked blindfolded. He carried a person on his back.

Philippe Petit has inspired many people. He walked between New York's World Trade Center towers. He did

Tightrope walkers started as entertainers.

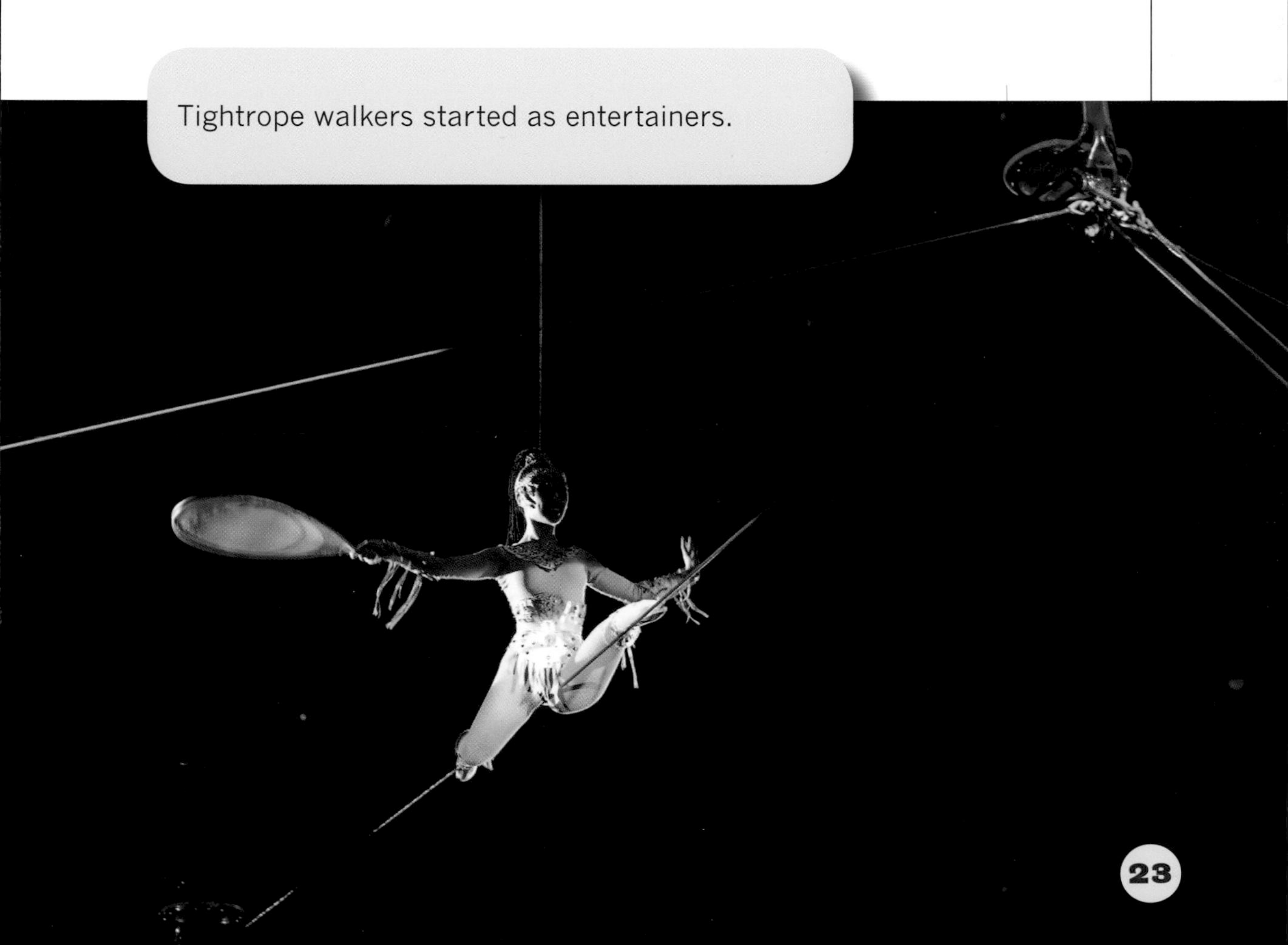

Many tightrope walkers are inspired by Philippe Petit. There's a film about him called *Man on Wire*.

this in 1974. It was called the "artistic crime of the century." Thousands watched him.

He was 1,350 feet (411.5 m) high. He walked over 200 feet (61 m). It took him 45 minutes. He danced. He lied down. He kneeled. He saluted watchers. He got off when it started to rain.

He faced challenges. The towers swayed. The weather was unstable. He broke laws. He sneaked past security guards. He had to get his gear to the rooftops. He planned for six years.

Extreme Tightrope Walking: Know the Lingo

Alfalfa: paper money in a circus

All out and over: the show is over and circus workers can start cleaning up

Back yard: dressing rooms of performers

Center of gravity: a single point where the object's weight is evenly placed

Gaucho: someone working in the circus who wasn't born into the circus

Guy wires: a cable used to add stability to a structure

Itchy feet: the urge to perform

King poles: poles longer than 36 feet (11 m) used for artificial high wire performances

Lot lice: children of circus performers and workers

Sag: the looseness in the line

Turnaway: a sold-out show

Under the stars: a show outside of a tent

5 More Than Walking

How do tightrope walkers make their sport more extreme?

Walking across a wire is not enough for some. Extreme tightrope walkers create challenges.

Jorge Ojeda-Guzman is from South America. He's a circus performer. He has a world record. He has the tightrope endurance record. He lived on a high wire. He did it for 205 days. He did it in Florida. He battled the heat. He battled a storm. He said, "It was kind of scary and it rained the whole night. I didn't sleep that night." A machine brought his family up to visit him. Supplies were brought up as well.

He came back down. But he didn't stay on the ground for

long. He left 15 minutes later. He went **bungee** jumping. A bungee is a long rubber rope. He dropped from a high place. He sprang 75 feet (23 m) into the air.

Jade Kindar-Martin biked across a 394-foot-high (120 m) wire. His wife was hanging below him. The wire was set between two warehouses in England. They were 89 feet (27 m) in the air. Their act is called "Bridging the Gap."

Mustafa Danger rode across a high wire on his motorcycle. He was in Spain. He was 610 feet (186 m) above the

Extreme tightrope walkers walk higher. They walk longer. They want more difficult walks.

When Extreme Is Too Extreme!

Faith Dickey practices highlining. It's an extreme sport. It combines rock climbing, slacklining, and tightrope walking. Highliners prefer bounce to tightness. Instead of wires and rope, they walk on nylon. Nylon is more stretchy. It swings. It bounces. It's thinner. It's more dangerous. For safety, some highliners use parachutes. Highliners balance using their arms. Dickey highlined in high heels and in the rain. The shoes were two sizes too big. She said, "It was extremely challenging. Some even thought impossible. ... Since no one had ever tried to walk a highline in high heels, I decided to try it. Highlining is so hard already, and walking in high heels isn't easy either. So combining them was very tricky." She has broken female highlining records. She did the highest free solo walk for a woman. She highlined 820 feet (250 m) above ground. She earned the longest highlining distance. She highlined 180 feet (55 m).

ground. He stopped after a few feet. He was pulled to safety. He was trying to break a world record. He wanted to go across 1,640 feet (500 m) without a safety net. He failed on his first try. But he tried again. He did it the second time.

Tightrope walkers are unstoppable.

Extreme tightrope walkers add tricks.

Did You Know?

- Tightrope walking is also called funambulism. It's Latin. *Funis* means "rope." *Ambulare* means "to walk."
- Osbert Humperdinck Pumpernickle is a dog. He holds a world record. He has the "Fastest Crossing of a Tightrope by a Dog." The tightrope was 11.4 feet (3.5 m). It took him 18.22 seconds.
- Tsovkra-1 is a village in Russia. Everyone walks tightrope. Tightroping is a tradition there. There's a legend about how it started. Young men got tired of walking across the mountain. They wanted to meet women in another village. The men put a rope across the valley. They built a shortcut.
- Chris Bull and Phoebe Baker were married on a wire. They were 80 feet (24 m) above their guests. Bull is a professional tightrope walker. Baker is a circus costume designer.
- Harold Barnes bounced on a tightrope. He was over a lake. He did flips. He sat down. He skipped with a rope. He slid backward. He was 12 years old.
- Joseph Gordon-Levitt played Philippe Petit. The movie is called *The Walk*. The actor trained with Petit for eight days. He learned to balance with a pole. Jade Kindar-Martin is his stunt double.

Consider This!

TAKE A POSITION! Learn more about Nik Wallenda's walk across Niagara Falls. Learn about Felix Baumgartner's space dive. What do you think is more impressive: walking across Niagara Falls on a tightrope or breaking the speed of sound in a skydive? Argue your point with reasons and evidence.

SAY WHAT? There are different types of tightrope walking. Describe each type. Explain how they are similar. Explain how they are different.

THINK ABOUT IT! Many believe tightrope walking is performance art. And, the audience is part of the act. Tightrope walkers believe that the audience members' fear is part of the thrill. It adds to the danger. What do you think about that?

SEE A DIFFERENT SIDE! Tightrope walkers need to consider their environments. They need to build strong and secure lines. This means they have to do things to buildings or nature. Freddy Nock took three years to get permission to tightrope between Swiss mountains. He couldn't damage the mountains. How do you think officials view tightrope walking?

Learn More: Resources

PRIMARY SOURCES

Man on Wire, a documentary about Philippe Petit (2008).

On a Tightrope, a documentary about Uyghur children learning how to tightrope walk (2007).

SECONDARY SOURCES

Gerstein, Mordicai. *The Man Who Walked Between the Towers*. Brookfield, CT: Roaring Brook Press, 2003.

Meinking, Mary. *Who Walks The Tightrope? Working at a Circus*. Chicago: Raintree, 2011.

WEB SITES

American Guild of Variety Artists: www.agvausa.com

Circus Fans Association of America: www.circusfans.org

World Acrobatics Society: www.worldacro.com

Glossary

acrobats (AK-ruh-bats) people who perform gymnastic-like stunts

architectural (ahr-ki-TEK-chur-uhl) buildings; high wire walking across buildings and other structures

artificial (ahr-tuh-FISH-uhl) man-made; high wire walking across distances created by poles like in a circus

braided (BRAYD-id) woven together

bungee (BUHN-jee) a rubber rope

circus (SUR-kuhs) a traveling show

high wire (HYE WIRE) walking on a tightrope in high places

natural (NACH-ur-uhl) made by nature; high wire walking across naturally occurring heights and distances

pyramid (PIR-uh-mid) a 3-D triangle

ravine (ruh-VEEN) a narrow canyon with steep slopes

slack (SLAK) loose

the big top (THUH BIG TAHP) the main circus tent where the big performances are held

Index